UNDOUBTED

Adriano Lecaldare

ISBN: 978-1-998662-37-1

Cover Design: Meredith Lindsay

Visit AOS Publishing's website:

www.aospublishing.com

A Collection of

Poetry and *Artwork*

Contents

Introduction

I have been writing since the age of nine, when I was diagnosed with a rare form of Leukemia that saw me spending a lot of time alone in a small room with nothing but my thoughts and dreams to keep me occupied.

My aunt visited one day and brought a blank journal, amongst other things, and suggested that I begin to write down my experience at the hospital, perhaps to cope with and understand what was happening to me. At first all I wrote were very straightforward accounts about what I did during the day. I began to realize that they were becoming stale and repetitive. I am not sure when the shift happened where I started to look inwards at my feelings and emotions instead of simply transcribing my immediate reality; however, this change unlocked within me the natural urge to express myself with words and writing.

I wrote my first self-proclaimed decent poem at sixteen years old in high school, titled *Who I Am* and have never stopped since. During my late teenage years and early adulthood, however, I found myself battling with addiction, which began directing and inspiring the content of my work, always leaning towards the light and trying to chase happiness despite how dark the world around me had become. I was interested in disassembling what I was feeling and reassembling it into words and poetry, with a natural tendency towards rhyming. I enjoy how writing can be a puzzle with language regarding how you place the words and what order can create a unique sound when read aloud.

The first part of the book deals with darker times in my life, whereas the second part is my change of direction, when I finally decided to reach out and ask for help and live my life choosing happiness and joy. I have picked out some of the poetry I have written through the years as a sort of journey through my life and what I was trying to understand about the world around me. I have always written with the intention of sharing my work, both on the written page and audibly through open mics and spoken word events in the hope that my words can help others who might be experiencing similar feelings and are trying to look for a light at the end of a long and dark tunnel. I write to better understand myself and in turn share my discoveries so that others may become aware of or relate to a certain feeling or thought. I encourage my readers to never give up, and when ready, to reach out and ask for help, for only you can do it, but you can't do it alone.

Part One

Who I Am

2009

People running up the street

Not looking at their feet.

People jumping up and down,

Not looking at the ground.

People running out of breath,

Not thinking about death.

People realize what's wrong—

It just makes them strong, but am I wrong?

For I have realized what is right,

And people go tell me to fly a kite.

I don't think that's too bright.

People telling me who I am,

Telling me I'm like a fan:

Always going around in circles,

Never seeing straight.

That's what I hate;

I hate when people discriminate.

They don't even look at the ground when

they jump.

One day they'll fall down,

And I'll stop turning 'round

And get up,

And all the things they said—

All that stuff will fall with them.

And I'll be that fan who can—

I'll be who I am.

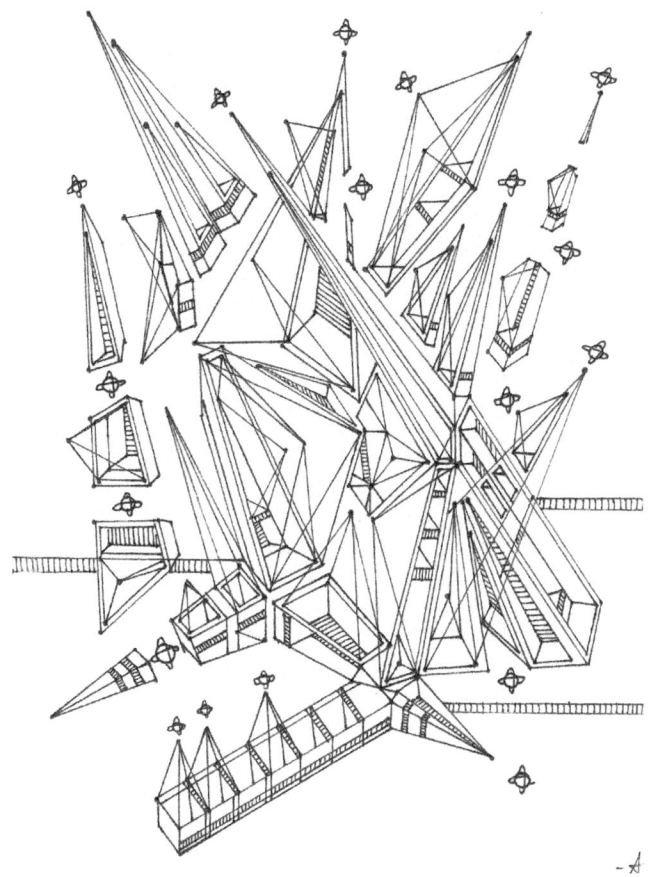

Back and Forth

01.29.16

Pacing back and forth

Back and forth

South and North

The needle on the compass simply reads,

Abort!

Get the heck out!

It won't matter which way you're going if you head in with Doubt.

Being lost in your thoughts offers plenty of solitude, and time in your mind—

However long alone, it'll prove difficult to find a different perspective.

Faced with a crossroad, so change direction

and head in willfully.

East and West

Proves another test,

Which only you can complete.

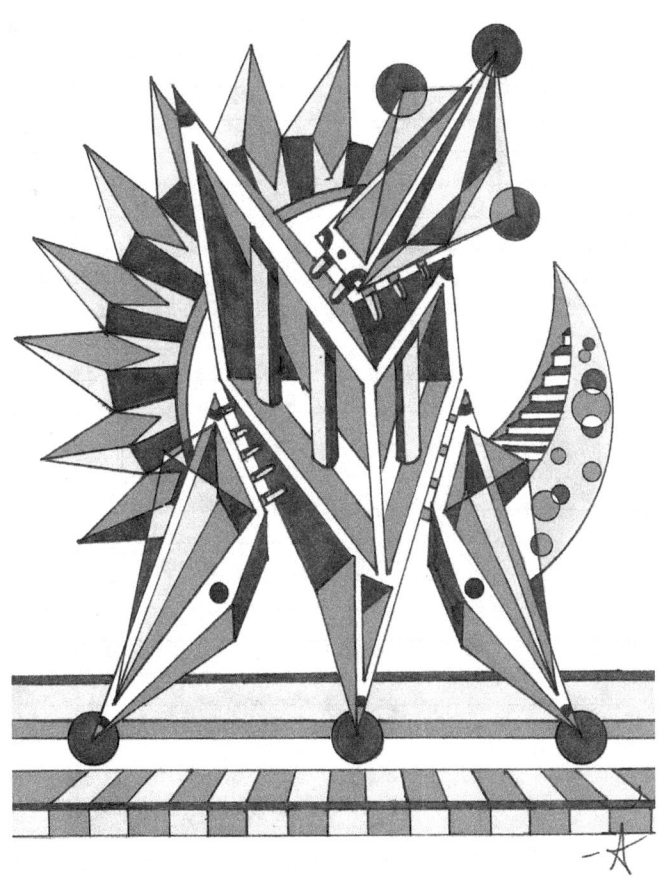

Fear of Landing

07.15.14

The fear of landing

Is like standing on your head,

Seeing upside down,

Not getting out of bed.

Stable? Sure.

Able?

Not without a steel cable

Pulling you down,

For in the clouds, you've started to drown.

So release some steam and cease to dream, prepare for landing and standing in-between,

Altitude is lowered, and roots sink in,

Creating the foundation for all to begin.

Short Fuse

11.13.14

I have a short fuse?

No kidding.

Good thing I'm not spitting fire;

Just don't get too close.

I'm a really good Liar,

And I burn to the touch

Yet I can't figure out why

I still care so much.

Structure

04.18.2023

Maintain equilibrium

To sustain, remain,

For life is wearisome and quick to drain your energy.

Create a structure and avoid the enemy that is procrastination,

Take a deep breath of relaxation

And be consistent in action.

Only one false step toward dissatisfaction.

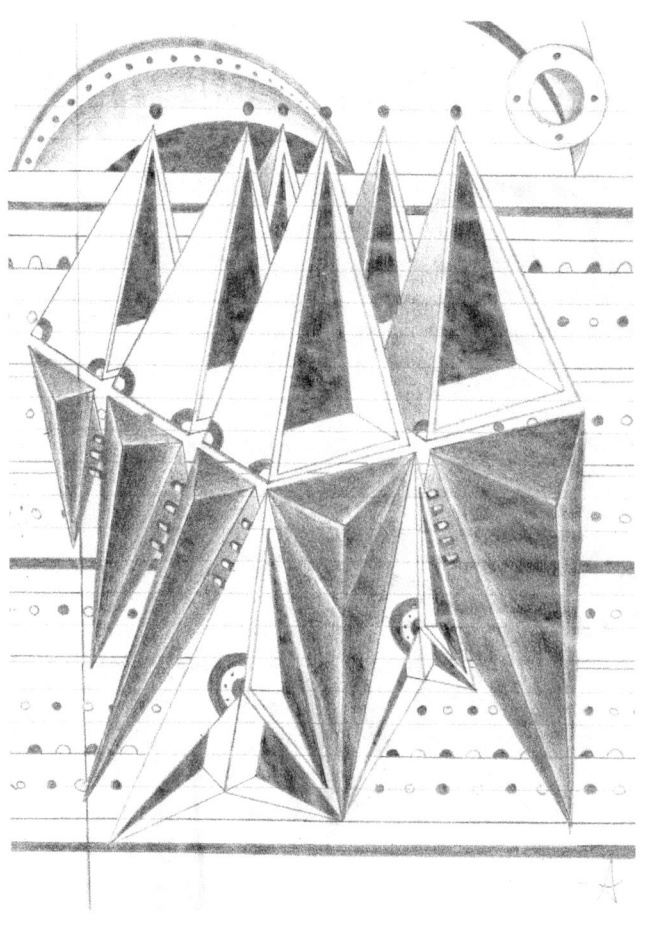

Never Alone

05.02.23

Break the cycle, remove the chains, dowse the darkness in scorching flames.

Down the barrier, crack the shell, find the counter to snap the spell.

Follow the light, crawl out of the hole, reclaim the life your misery stole.

Eliminate the pain, abolish the anger, leave your worries to dry out on a hanger.

Lighten the load, find support in others; you are never alone, nor the only one who suffers.

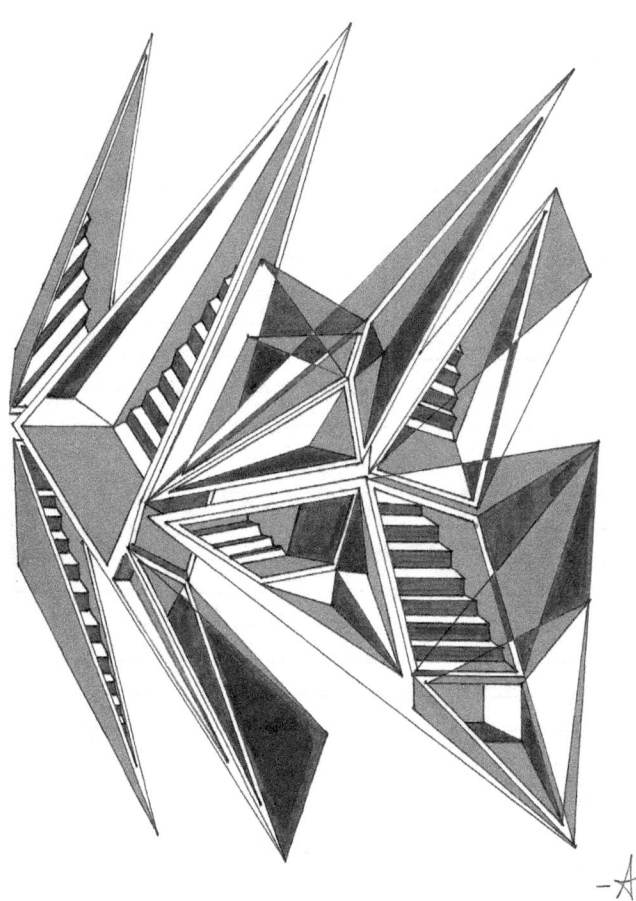

Hollowing Distances

02.22.18

Unidentified,

They combine to form unspecified memories

Of times I cannot entirely remember.

They assemble and reform fragmented instances

Only to break apart,

Hollowing distances.

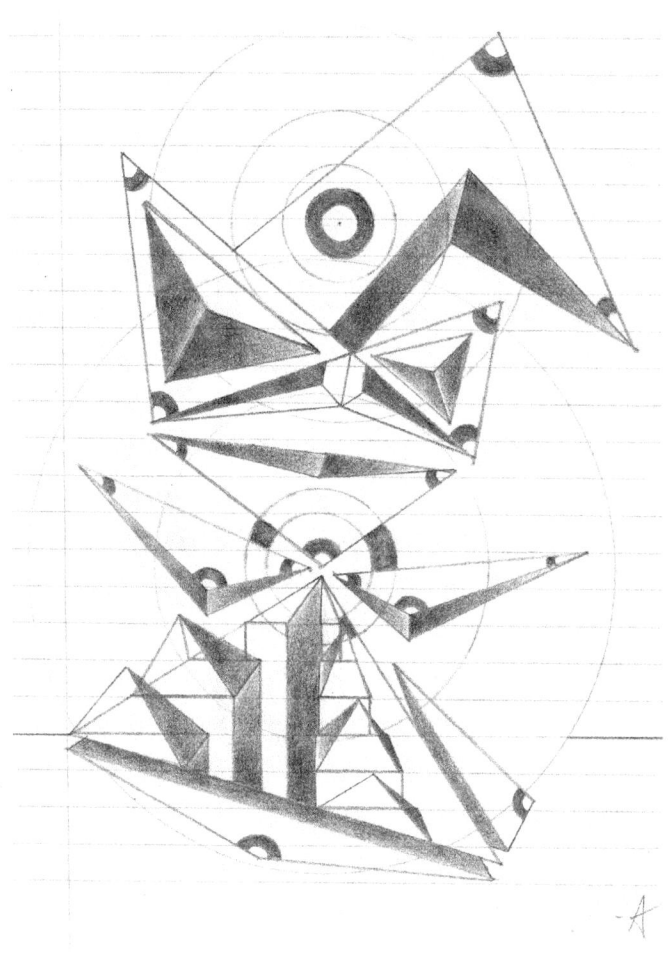

Programmed

04.28.23

In moments of doubt and times of worry, your body is programmed to run away, scurry, find a dark place, and cower in fear

Of all the good things you've been trained not to hear.

A time will come when enough is enough, and you will need to unburden your mind of this bluff

The lies that you've held, the numerous thoughts of joy expelled.

To uncage your heart, remember a way to find a new start and language to say,

You are worth every bit, the whole package as well. How long will it take? Only time will tell.

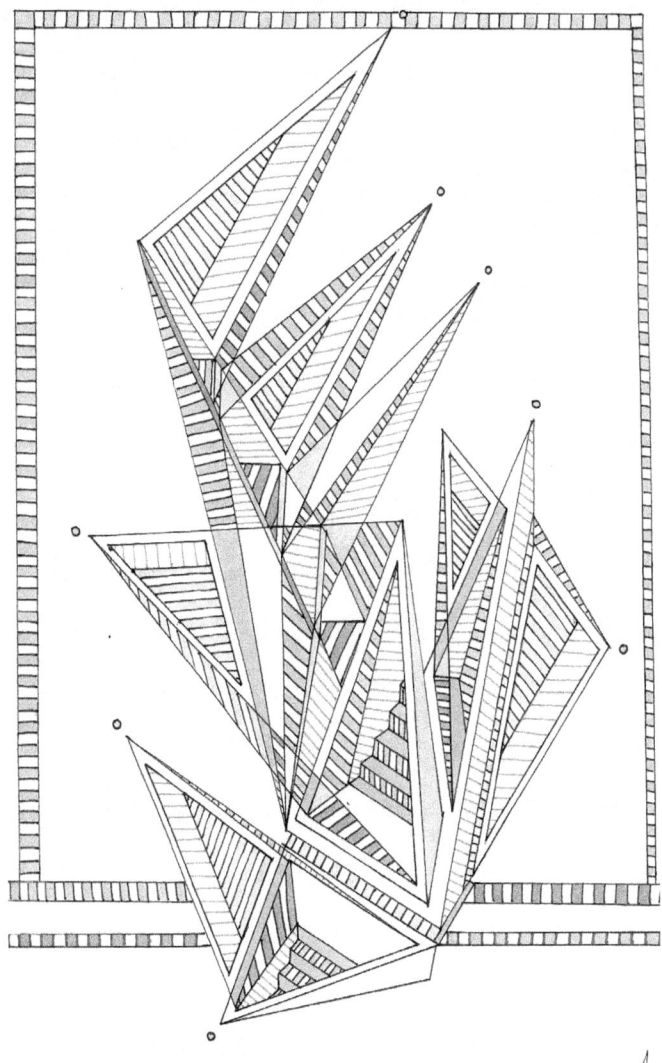

- A

Moving Past the Past

01.28.19

Trying to get by,

Moving past the past

Onto the future, but not so fast.

If you skip a step, it might not last.

It may crack,

Break apart—

Many little pieces make it difficult to restart.

Honesty

2016

Self-control

Introspection

Always speak with good intention,

Not to mention honesty

Then the truth will set you free.

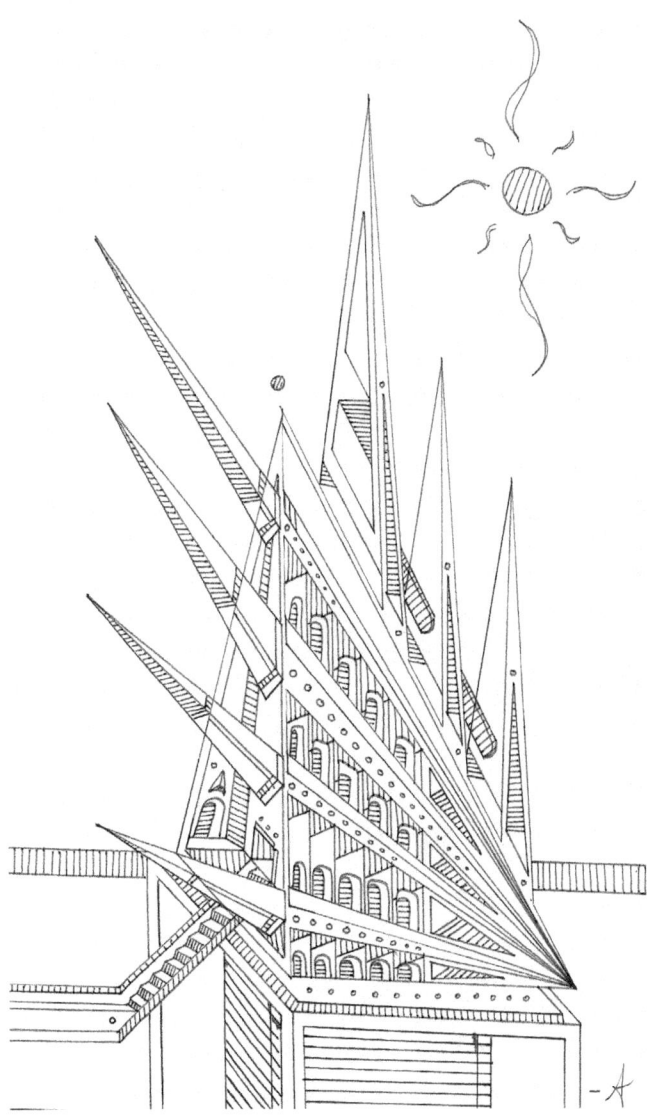

Lead On

04.17.17

What could possibly be the direction when

Switching track,

As a last-second decision,

Grinding the rails

Without major precision,

Or simply plowing through

And allowing someone else to

Take the reigns,

Direct and orient runaway trains.

When going for a ride

To an unknown location,

Being shown

Different paths of variation

Offers new roads and outcomes,

Without some of which

I wouldn't still be leading on.

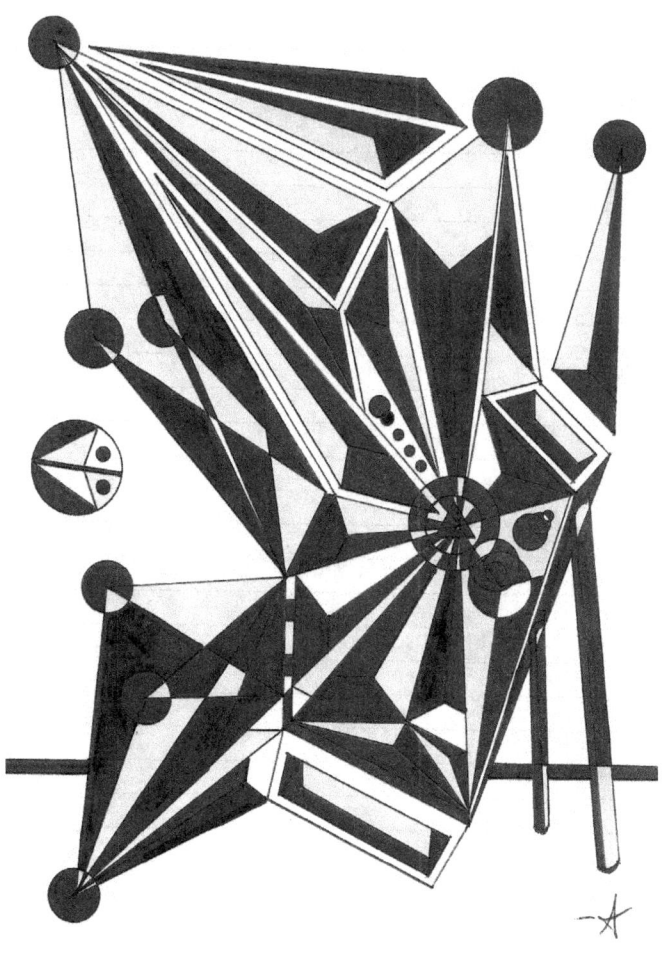

Straight Thoughts

04.13.17

When alone

And sharing thoughts only with yourself,

Past and Present

Seem to meld.

The Future is shown,

Held behind transparent glass—

See-through

All the way to the very last

Pain.

Drain the excess

That which won't be absorbed,

And focus your mind;

Straight thoughts are difficult

To form,

To find.

Next Target

02.07.17

Taken seriously, I can bend steel with my mind,

Mysteriously send energy through space and time.

However, it doesn't seem to be the case,

For all I say is easily Erased from memory;

Swiftly escaping, they still weigh heavily,

Sinking through the ground,

Plunging deeper,

Waiting to be found.

So I'll take my shovel when tossed to the dirt,

Pick them back up and reassert my will.

Find the next target and go in for the Kill.

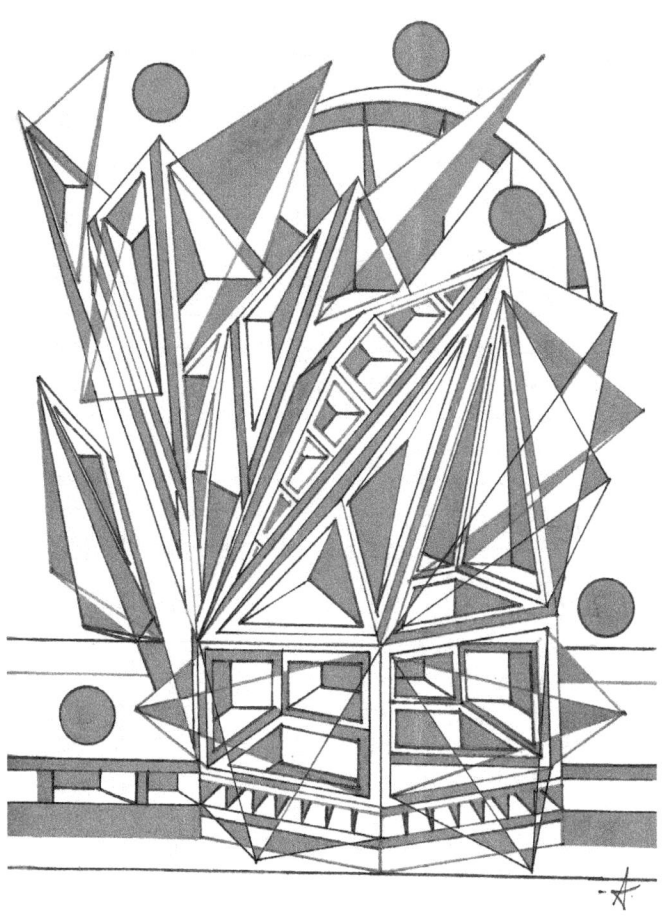

Rabbit Hole

04.22-27.23

One thought leads to the next, and the next thing you know,

Down the rabbit hole, further down you go

There's no end

You'd best look out below, 'cause rock bottom's just the top,

And you've trodden in the clutter as you finish with this mutter in your head, you wonder why instead,

One thought leads to the next, and the next, and the next thing you know…

To Depart

You stop to think, yet feel instead,

Then realize

It's in your Heart,

It's in your Head,

No better place to find a start,

So

Get out of bed

To depart

Trust me now, I'm really smart.

Sixty-Six Home

09.30.14

It started off all so wrong

To me— a task, are you Weak or Strong?

Survive despite the world around,

Pick yourself up from the cold hard ground.

Alive? Alright,

Now hear my voice

I speak of this because I have no choice.

No matter how grim it seems, as long as you have dreams,

I am always here to help.

But the toughest part,

You must deal with yourself.

Without Compromise

12.30.16

A brief slip was more than enough to tip the scales—

Only two possible outcomes,

Yet I can't seem to make heads or tails

Of the problem at hand.

If only there was another way to understand

These feelings,

But I'm left out, dealing in the dark,

Wandering aimlessly, trying to find a spark

To ignite the flame

It's been so long, quenched in rain

Dims the light, lessens the heat

Leaving one to back away, retreat

From fear and loss

And leave the Desire to carry on to a coin toss.

Whether easy or difficult to make it through the day,

Endure without compromise

Of any other way.

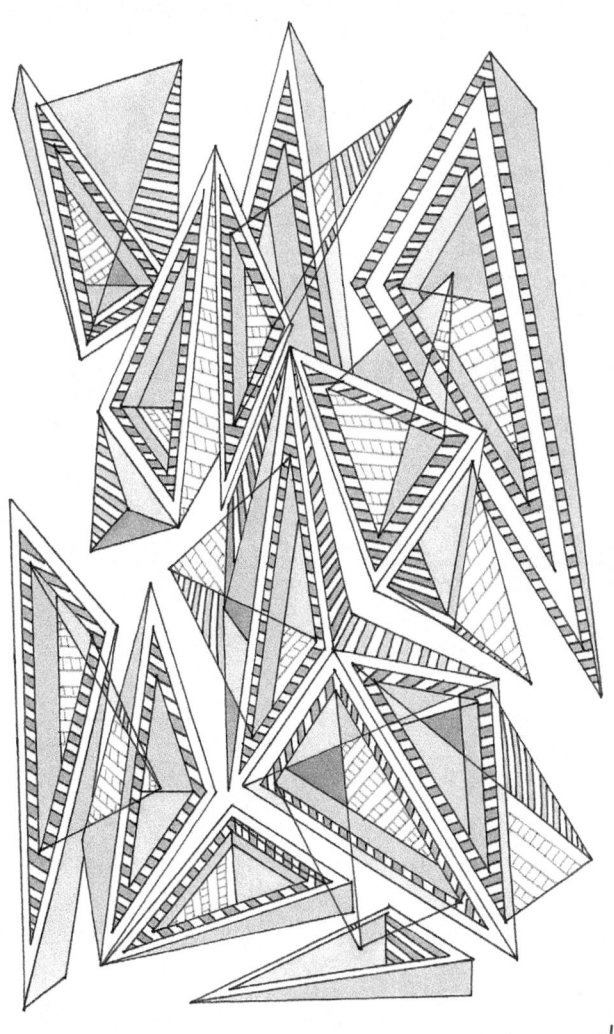

-A

Next Time

04.17.23

How many ways have you said,

"Next time"?

So many days that you've felt just fine telling yourself you will do it later,

Only to trip and fall in a crater.

Light yourself up over an open fire and forget about the promise you made,

As the next time came and went

To the same place all your lies were sent.

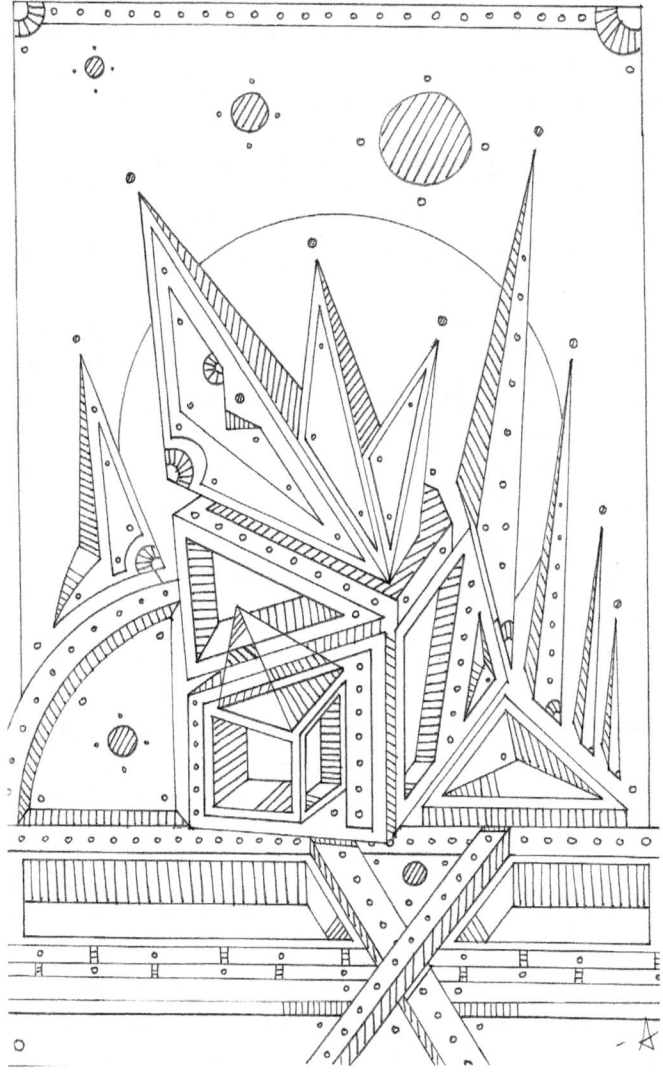

Exposed

04.20.23

Exposed and vulnerable, I'm supposed to be wonderful,

Yet the armor was shed, and I'm left feeling half-dead.

Frail and Fragile, let's bail; I'm quite agile when I need to run away,

Go get lost and have fun some other way.

Deep dive into thoughts, sleep deprivation provides lots of time to wander into feelings

While exposed, holding in, reeling,

All there's left to do is let go

No point in going against the flow to get carried away;

Submit to the current and have yourself a nice day.

Unalive

04.20-26.23

Every sip I take, every puff, sniff, or shake, I depreciate who I am, who I can be.

The very possibility is stolen when I'm free to choose, and choose to lose, run, or scare, hide and abuse.

I might as well be unaware, unalive, just stop and quit, don't even try.

Who are you to me? At what point did you run free in my head, take control, toss aside, down the hole?

Every sip I take, every puff, sniff or shake, I depreciate who I am, who I can be.

The very possibility is stolen when I'm free to choose, and choose to lose, run or scare, hide and abuse.

I might as well be unaware, unalive, just stop and quit, don't even try.

Why are you here, tempting me with nothing? Fear took over, leaving me with something to pretend, down the street, around the bend, gun waiting, ready to send me to heaven, where leaving me replevin.

Keep asking the question, why is it that when I'm at the top, the only thing before me is a mountainous drop?

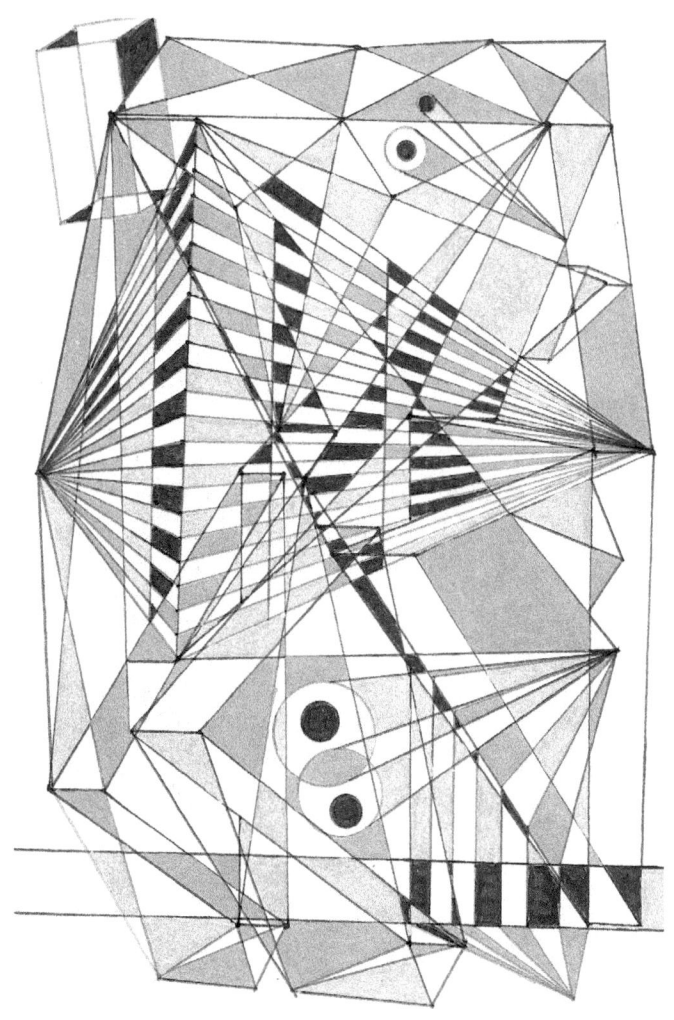

Part Two

Lac Echo

06/01/23

Shimmers in the wind, the deep waters within

Ripples in the pond from wherever they've been,

Can't explain the feeling of wondering why my thoughts drift away to an empty sky.

Release some steam, untie the knot, defy the fear the net has caught

My floating dreams pierced between blinding beams of light

Burn the anger through a cool calm night.

A lake of worry flooded the truth;

If I don't hurry,

Time's absolute.

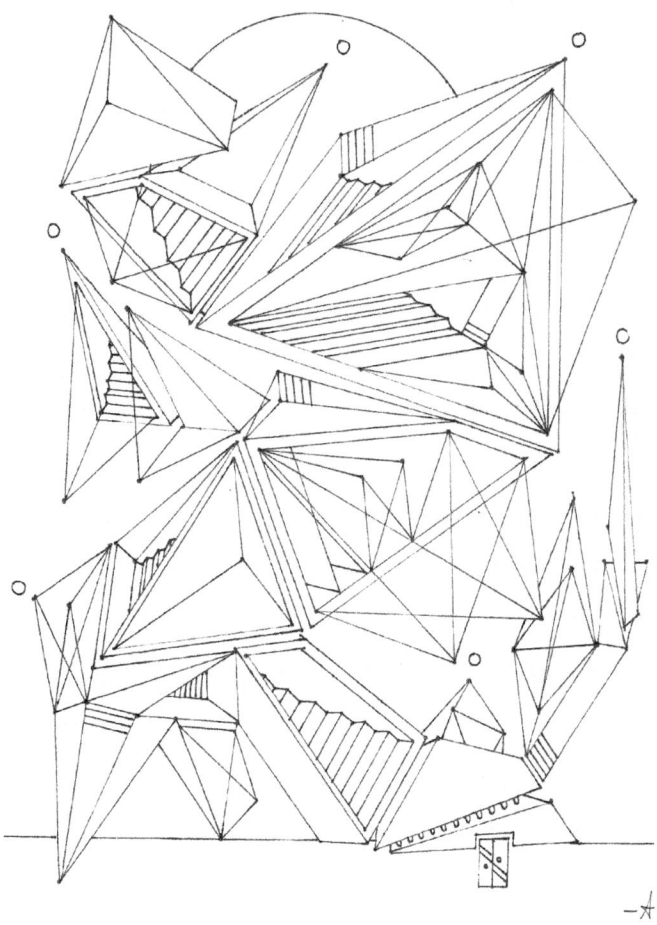

Heaven and Hell

06/11/23

Knowing and doing, going and proving yourself,

Growing and moving, through Heaven and Hell.

Showing your heart and going past the end, knowing the start is just around the bend,

So with a pen I send, then letting the words continue spreading on the page, remembering when they were full of guilt and rage

Built to cage the beast, gauge the heat, too cold to beat it back, always continue to pierce the lack of and crack the shell, when coming and going through Heaven and Hell.

Squander Time

06/14/23

Empty the void, unthink the mind, unreel the heart, and nothing I'll find to,

or blind me from my reflection

Bind me to a moment of dissatisfaction, treadles and lacking traction, headless without direction, heartless,

A broken-apart mess of thick and thin and nothing within, without something of any amount,

but the one thing I never had; a love so strong that I could never be glad of myself.

Being someone else that had to tell a lie, just to squander time and move on by, ponder why

I chose to strain

my essence down an empty drain.

Lac Echo #2

Sparkling specks of white light

Dotting the water paints a speechless sight,

Reaching farther, so bright

They sting my soul, comfort my mind

As the splashing waves help to find the way back

And rising yells don't fail to track the sounds of joy

Of lives of men trying to find the boy they've all let go,

A desperate attempt to live and grow past a crumpled clock,

As I lay and rest on the floating dock of dreams,

Anchored in place,

Battered by beams of sun, while I decide the time

When it begins

And how it's done.

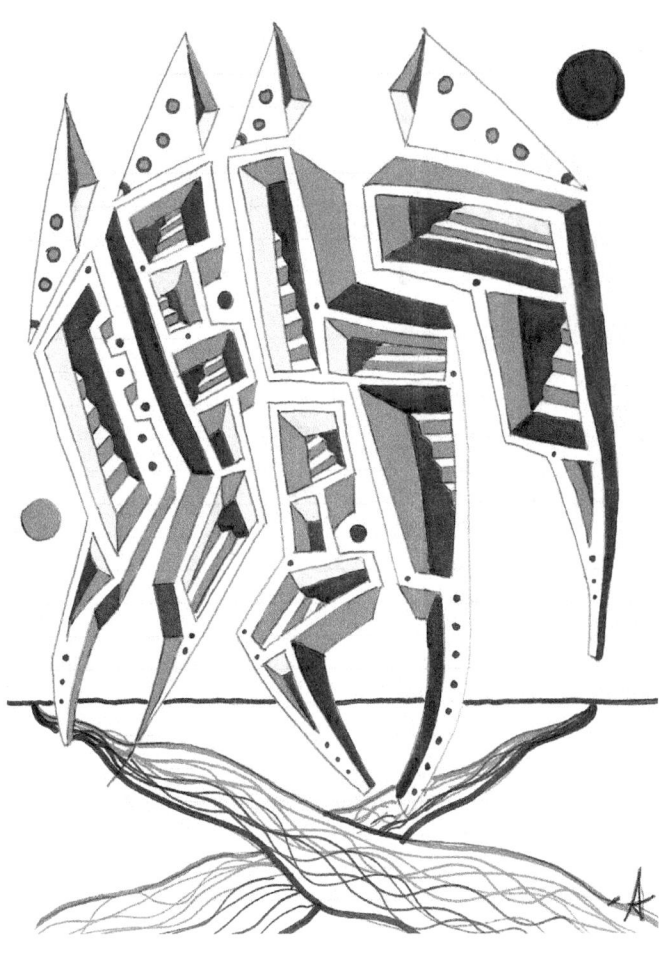

Lac Echo #3

06.22.23

Let's take our time, by the lake,

And make a rhyme while we bake

Under the midway sun,

Halfway there, the day's almost done

As we float above the water,

Just don't drift away farther than the eye can see,

As I wonder why we didn't do this sooner.

Softer breeze rustles leaves nearby,

And dragonflies, bees, and cries of yes and please carried by the lake

It takes moments to hear and seconds to forget the sound,

The pain, and regret, and drain the darkness in light,

Harness the bright sun,

Whatever said but now done,

Bled, but now one with myself

Instead

Incoming the new,

And paddle away with this quiet canoe.

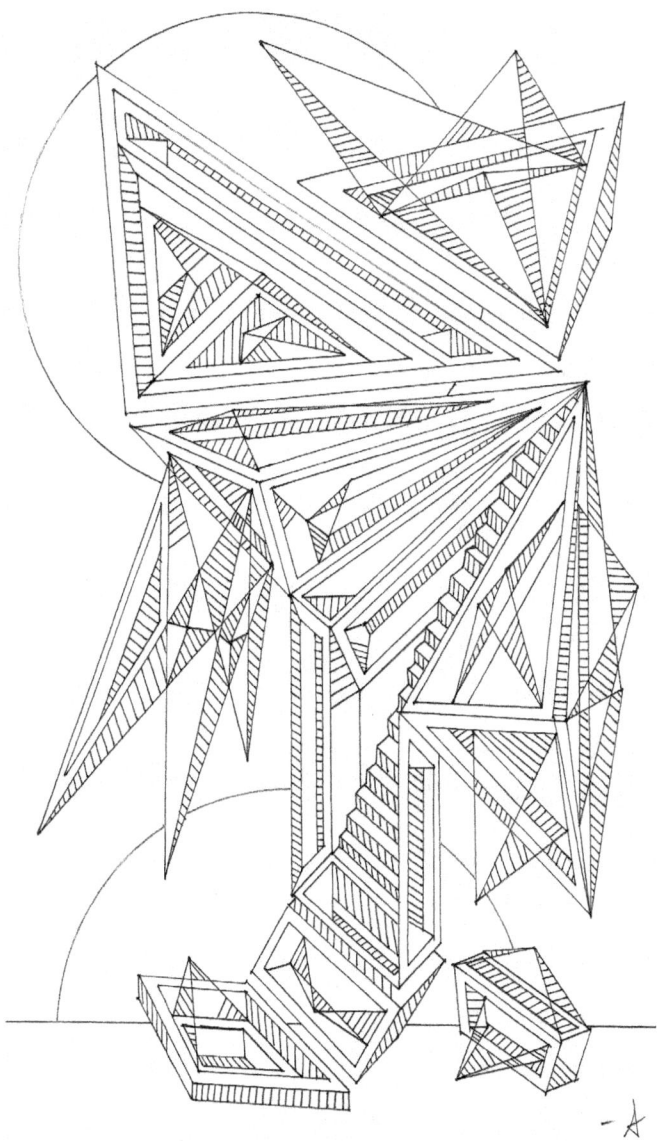

Pressure

06.24.23

Too much pressure,

Pent up, bent out of shape,

Feeling spent out, like rent's up, charging a high amount,

There's no Escape,

Building, stacking, compressing, compounding,

Resonating in my head

Too much pressure

Pushing,

Now I'm fed up, feeling dead

Inside, bled and dried out,

Dread and drained, tied down and blamed,

A rising rate amassing,

Surpassing the limit, breaking the needle

Taking the feeble frame, to weed out and tame

The wild growth getting out of hand

Too much pressure

And overstock demand

Will pop the lid, at one point drop and rid,

Put a stop and stand up, mop up the mess,

Confess your sins

Ease up and squeeze out the pain

Too much pressure

Before you go insane.

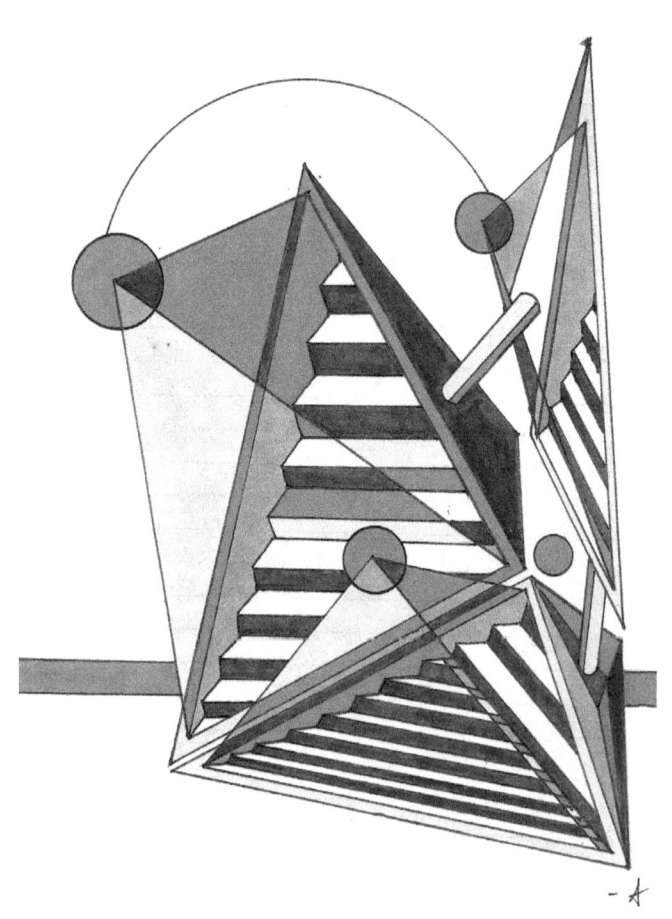

Lac Echo #4

06.24.23

Grey and humid, thoughts stray and foggy

At bay, mind groggy as it dips in and out of the water,

Trips out farther on soggy soil,

Wet footsteps spoil

Dry dirt beneath, while my hurt

Seeps, tepid, decrepit, somewhat expected behavior

Flotation device and no Savior to savor the moment,

Too far out, a distant opponent splashes and dashes for the exit

On this cloudy and rowdy day, pouting and doubting my misery away.

No fun anymore, not one but more, and no sun but shore—

Sharp rocks explore each step below, as nature cries and I hide alone.

Lac Echo #5

06.27.23

Sitting on a well, just listening,

Caught in a spell, wishing to tell you how I feel

Stuck in place wondering what is real and what is true

How to heal and what to do.

Things you knew and what would fit,

Like sitting on a well, and bit by bit,

Hitting the nail on the head,

Reaching for the light above.

Instead of crying about it,

Of lying and trying to cover it up,

Unsealing the lid and filling the cup with as much as you need,

Draining the excess and staying up to speed,

Cleaning up the mess

To climb out and succeed.

Fear of Fear

06.29.23

Fear of Fear itself—

Holding dear to the churning gears of Hell,

Steer not into frozen plains, the endless rains of worry,

Or bury the light beneath thick sheets and cover your sight deep within,

Where seeping fright speaks lies and tries to sway the balance

In and out of conjured allowance

To get lost in the void

Where frost and cold have toyed with your mind,

Enjoyed control for too long,

Making it difficult to find a path, where fear takes over

And becomes the Fear itself, it spells disaster.

Rather than steal away and miss a moment,

Becoming your worst opponent,

Choose to win and change instead

After all

It's only in your head.

Breathe Free

07.02.23

I can breathe free, see past the veil,

As the sun shines through leaves

And birds sing between trees

I cannot fail.

Being here in the now,

Released from the past, which framed who I was

Not lost in the future and the wonder of how,

But here in the present and all that matters.

After or before won't affect this pleasant feel of the wind

Or beat of my heart,

Within or without thought,

To have been or have not

But to simply be

Clearly see the way, listen to my soul and the wonders at play

Before time decides the end—

I can breathe free,

Not knowing when.

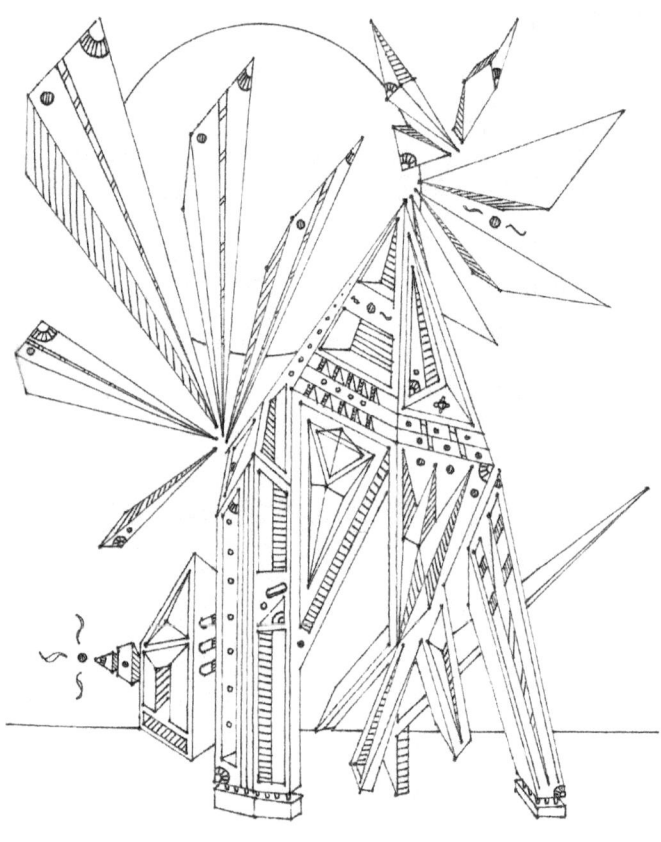

Danger Zone

07.12.23

It's a danger zone, a deep dark place where strangers roam

And scurry about

With hurry and doubt.

Being all alone in worry without aim,

All blurry, each day's the same

A mind drains, flurry and drought dry great plains

And lakes of life for strife,

Of joy for pain

In the danger zone,

There's nothing to gain.

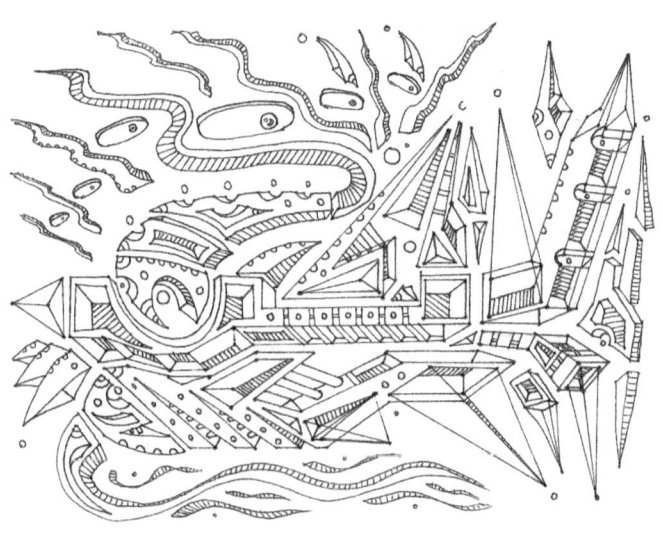

Take Time to Heal

07.16.23

Breach the broken seal

Where too deep the wound reveals the Root.

It squeals in pain, it deals with fear the same,

It feels the rain pound the roof to seek the leak

And drain,

To fill the room, flood in disdain

The mud rolls (over),

A mold for the former,

To hold back the lid,

Peel off the road block

And just be rid of pain and grief and give your brain the relief it needs

To breach the broken seal;

Take time to remind, remain, and heal.

On Trial

07.22.23

I went somewhere I haven't been for a while,

A burning witch trial where I pitched the torch in denial of myself

And what I felt churning inside,

Throwing my curses as I tried to hide from an angry crowd sending nothing but love.

I thought I was done there, and seeing the results after joining that occult life,

Of praising strife and grief and living in disbelief.

The flames rage on and I keep stoking the fire;

I enrage the trapped beast with the sole desire of disturbing the water.

My heart cries tears of pain as my mouth stays shut and continues playing games with my head.

It hurts so much

I can't go back

For my soul, my life, it's my choice to act.

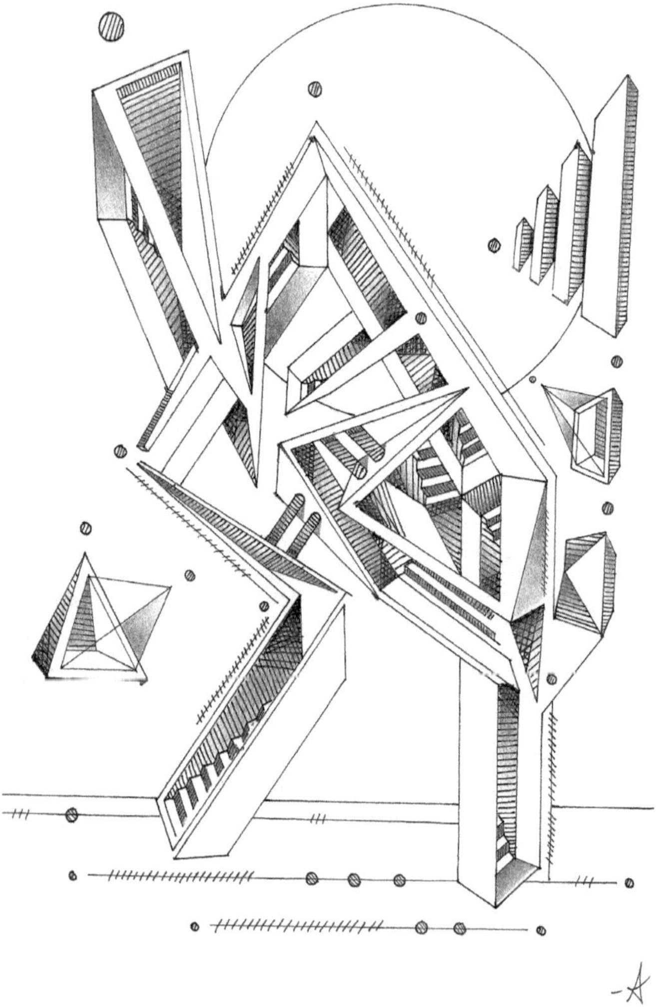

Tomorrow or Today

07.23.23

I wonder where I'm going to go when I have nowhere in sight,

Where there's no sun, no brilliant light

To guide me through the darkness.

I wander through the forest in search of what I can,

Because I know I am a beacon when all is Dark and Dim

Ignite the spark within my soul to help me carry on

Remember the joy of times I had that seemed too far and gone

And if I lose the path,

Trust in myself and all of those who believe that I can.

I am more than worthy now to find that happy day

Where birds will sing and sun will shine with no choice but to stay—

I will be the person who never gives up,

Whether it be tomorrow or today.

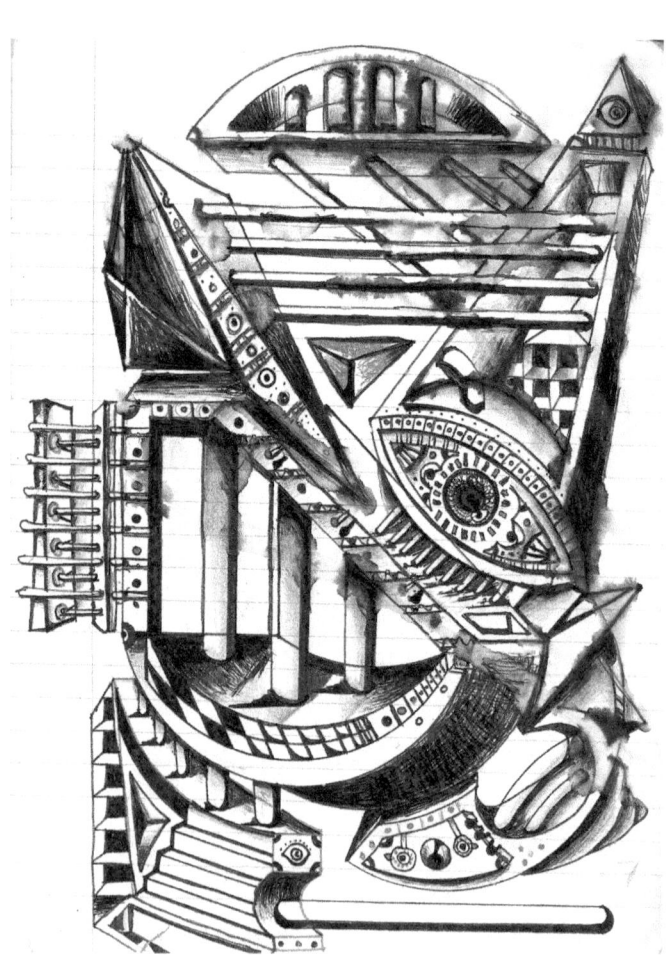

Camping #1

07.24.23

Inside-out,

I hide without cover

From raindrops as they stop,

And start.

I wonder where I am and how I've been,

What I feel that boils within as I chill out under the open sky

Water rushes quickly nearby, filling my mind,

Leaving my body behind to fend off the night

Where insects cling to hanging lights, searching for a path,

With nowhere to go but bathe in the twitching torch's wrath

As it flickers on

And I linger long past the sun,

My eyes wide open;

For all I know,

It has already been said and done.

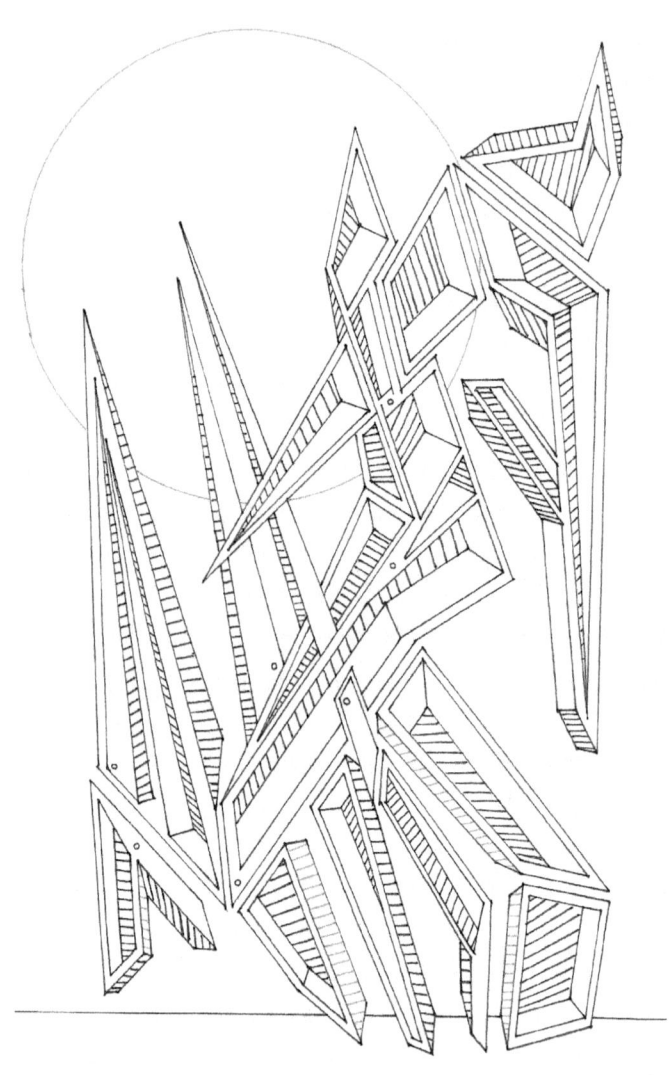

Camping #3

07.26.23

Through green trees, I see

More space than leaves

No place to please the quiet I find inside my mind

When my head isn't here.

Listen to the rain fall near my thoughts as each drop brings a reason to carry on,

A feeling to remember, for as long as I stay strong and true,

Links and ties both remain and remind me of where I am,

And that I can in fact find joy this day.

Despite the pain and fear that tries to snuff out the fire,

We trek the path,

And keep climbing higher.

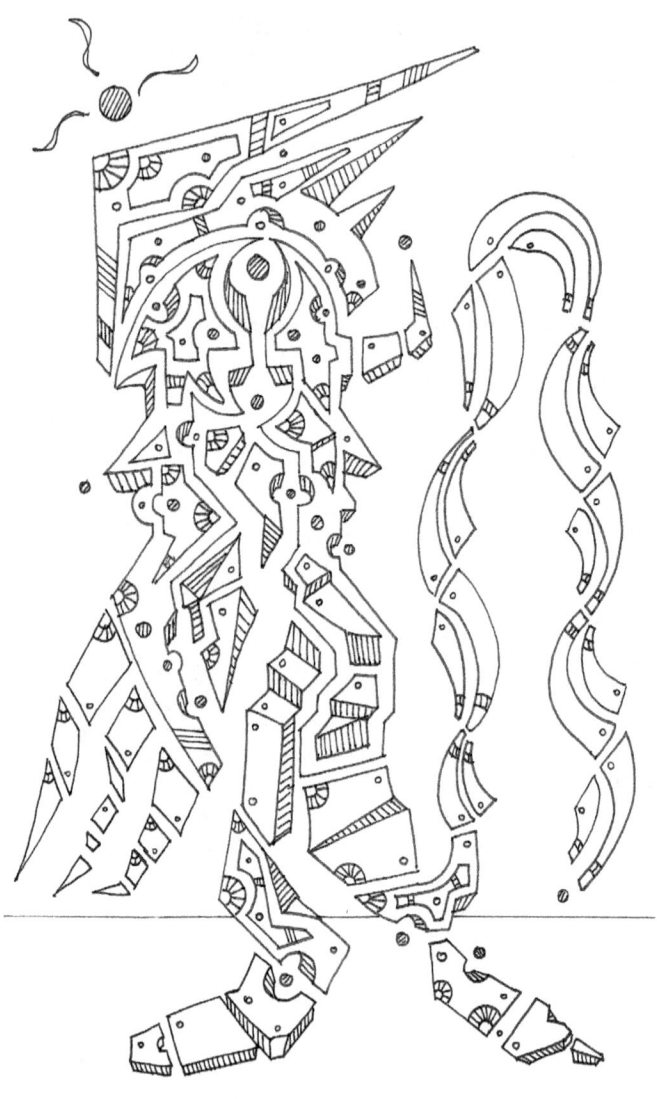

Bittersweet

07.30.23

Tasting bittersweet, this rich dessert was a welcome treat

To indulge the senses,

Relieve some pent-up stress, and lower my defenses,

Train my mind to not plunge into the future,

Or sink in memories gone;

To be here right now, hold dear to knowing how

To manage what I can and accept what's out of my hands,

To plan and prepare for things to go, and some to not,

Times to grow, and others to get caught.

How to untangle the web,

To live my life outside of my head,

And by using my heart,

Reclaim the moment, and begin at the start.

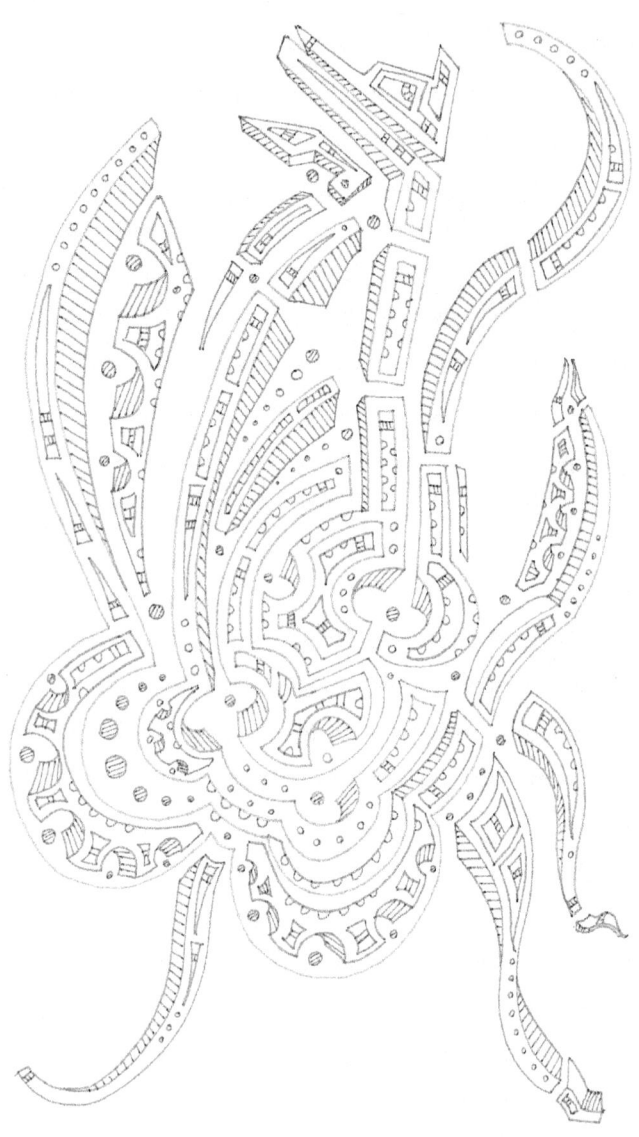

Fog

08.17.23

Fog sets in and I can't see past the veil— the mist is thick,

Too deep to tell the difference between the water and the sky, the ripples in the lake are all that move by my eyes.

Too clouded to distinguish why I chose to freeze time and hide behind a shroud of lies

To linger within my mind, constructing thoughts in a void of my own demise.

This wind blows through so high, lifting the curtain, clearing, dissolving the burden, dissipating like a dream.

From dense perceptions to ephemeral steam, steady as the water.

Doubt breaks apart and sight is carried farther, giving joy a place.

The fog is lifted, and I see my face in the reflection.

I accept who I am

And never change direction.

Goodnight

06.04.23

Looking outside, without a doubt, no matter how much wondering about when I'll snap out of this dream, my soul's been caged up, enraged, it screams to be free.

I brandish the weapon to escape destiny and run away from the truth that has always been me. There's nobody else; there's no better way to say I'm sorry, to lay it to rest and quit worrying.

I've been hiding inside for a while. I died without a death, my body was moving with every breath; my head had thoughts too quick to forget the pain.

My heart was still and void, drained and toyed with; no big brain could enjoy the love. I've been pushed back and beaten, mushed and compacted, with drink and without reason,

With smoke and fog, a toke to toggle the setting, and in the end only upsetting all the joy that tried to come in. I myself choosing not to win a game of my own making, forsaking my being,

Mistaking my time and running away. Seeing a losing battle, putting down my arms and chose not to rattle the cage, performing my lies on an empty stage, with no tickets for sale, a load of stale bread left, a male bereft of inner will, who despite all the passion, chose to cower still.

So now's not the time to continue down a road, a street that isn't new, or isn't cheap, but full of twists and turns,

For as vodka burns my dreams to dust, I trust my spirit more, and as drugs rob me of my precious life, I have so much in store.

I'll walk through flames before I let my steps lead me astray, I'll become the man I always said I'd love to be someday, and I'll choose to give my all to the uncertainty of time,

Say goodbye and pick myself up after each and every fall.

I am who I need to be and have always been at that, I'm more than enough, so no more falling in the endless trap of being lost in plain sight.

The way is clear, the path is lit, and to you I say goodnight.

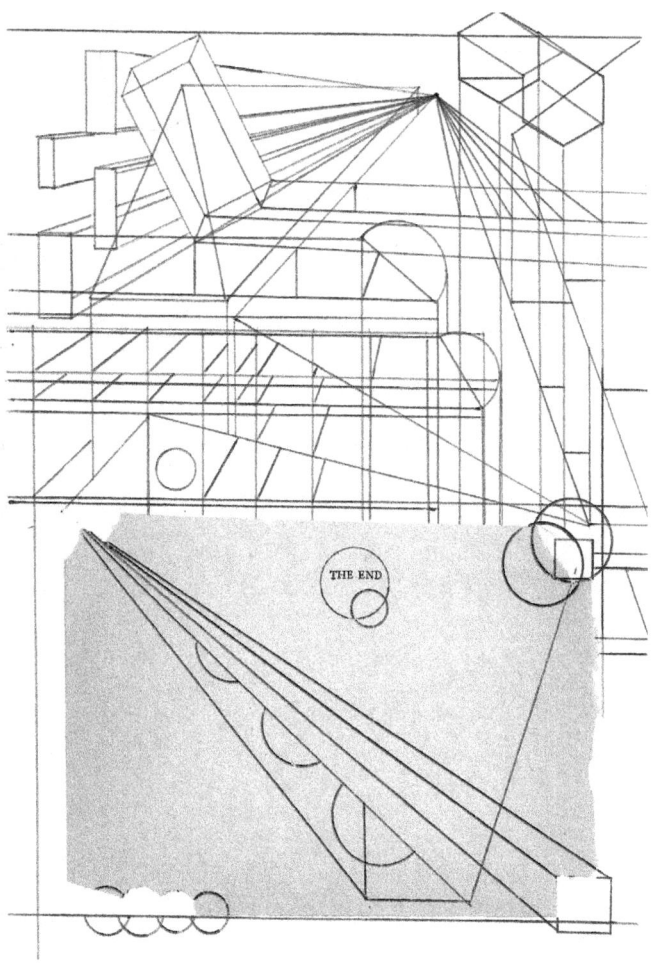

THE END